MW01716870

Animal Tracks

An Alphabet Coloring Book Filled With Facts And Poetry

To Dustin,
We hope that you enjoy our book
Mary Ellen Taylor

by Mary Ellen Taylor
with Kirsten and Zachary Lowe

Animal Tracks
Mary Ellen Taylor

ISBN 1-930052-33-2
Library of Congress Number 2006925330

Cherokee Books, 231 Meadow Ridge Pkwy, Dover, DE 19904

Foreword

When families live far apart, as many do in today's world, maintaining close bonds with grandchildren can be a challenge for grandparents. Our family is no exception because our daughter Donya is married to an Air Force officer. She and her husband Lt. Colonel David Lowe along with their four children, Kirsten, Zachary, Nathan, and Josiah have been stationed throughout the United States. Their military homes have included seven states. Our time spent together has been limited to one or two short visits a year. I realized that my husband Ed and I would not have the benefit of watching the grandchildren's personalities develop as their bodies grew. We needed a plan to help bridge this gap in miles.

As an English teacher, I value writing as a means of expression and recording of understanding of new concepts. The idea for Animal Tracks came about through a desire to create a long-term project that would be educational for the children and would create a bond between us. The book took several years to write and illustrate. We communicated via e-mail, US Mail, telephone, and in person during yearly visits. We divided up tasks. We conducted mini-writers' workshops while discussing our progress and critiquing one another's work. We laughed and worked hard.

Frequently selecting unusual animals, Kirsten (age 13) researched facts and wrote brief reports. I taught her citation writing, sentence combining, and other writing strategies. Observing her technical skills mature and her writing voice develop over years was a joy.

Her oldest brother Zachary (age 10) put his artistic abilities to work and created illustrations of each of the animals. A perfectionist, he often recreated pictures because he felt he could do better. His persistence was admirable.

I contributed short, light-hearted poetic pieces to accompany the illustrations. The rhymes also contain a lesson in alliteration. During one of our conversations, the children asked that I revisit my poem about vampire bat because they felt it was too silly. They didn't find bats at all amusing. Through writing this book, we were true collaborating writers and illustrators.

The two youngest boys, Nathan (7) and Josiah (6) contributed as well. Through dictation, they told about two favorite animals and made illustrations. Perhaps their work will be the beginning of a sequel to this book. Their contributions appear at the end of the book.

Finally, Animal Tracks would never have been completed without the loving, consistent devotion of their mother Donya. As a home schooling mother, she dedicated hours of encouragement and Christian guidance so that the children could complete their tasks. Through her overseeing of the project, the children learned organization and persistence along with valuable information about the animal world.

We hope that this book will serve as a model while encouraging other grandparents to reach out to their grandchildren to create a life-long bond through writing and illustrating a special book.

Mary Ellen Taylor 2006

Anteater

Many anteaters live in South America. Some enjoy living on the ground while others prefer trees for their homes. Anteaters are mammals with no teeth. Another interesting fact is that they walk on the sides of their feet. Just like their name says, they really like to eat ants by using their long snouts and long sticky tongues. Termites also are part of their food supply. Anteaters would be handy to take on a picnic to keep the ants away.

"Anteater." The World Book Student Discovery Encyclopedia. 2000. Vol. 1. p. 92.

Andy Anteater thinks nothing is sweeter than munching and crunching with his long-nosed feeder.

Barracuda

Barracudas are a type of fish with thin bodies and very sharp teeth. Twenty different kinds of barracudas can be found in the Atlantic, Indian, and Western Pacific Oceans. These fish can grow to be as long as six feet, and they can weigh up to one hundred pounds. Their diet consists of other fish. Here is a warning! People who go skin diving and snorkeling should stay away from barracudas because these fish can be very dangerous.

"Barracuda." The World Book Student Discovery Encyclopedia. Vol. 2. 2000. p. 25.

B

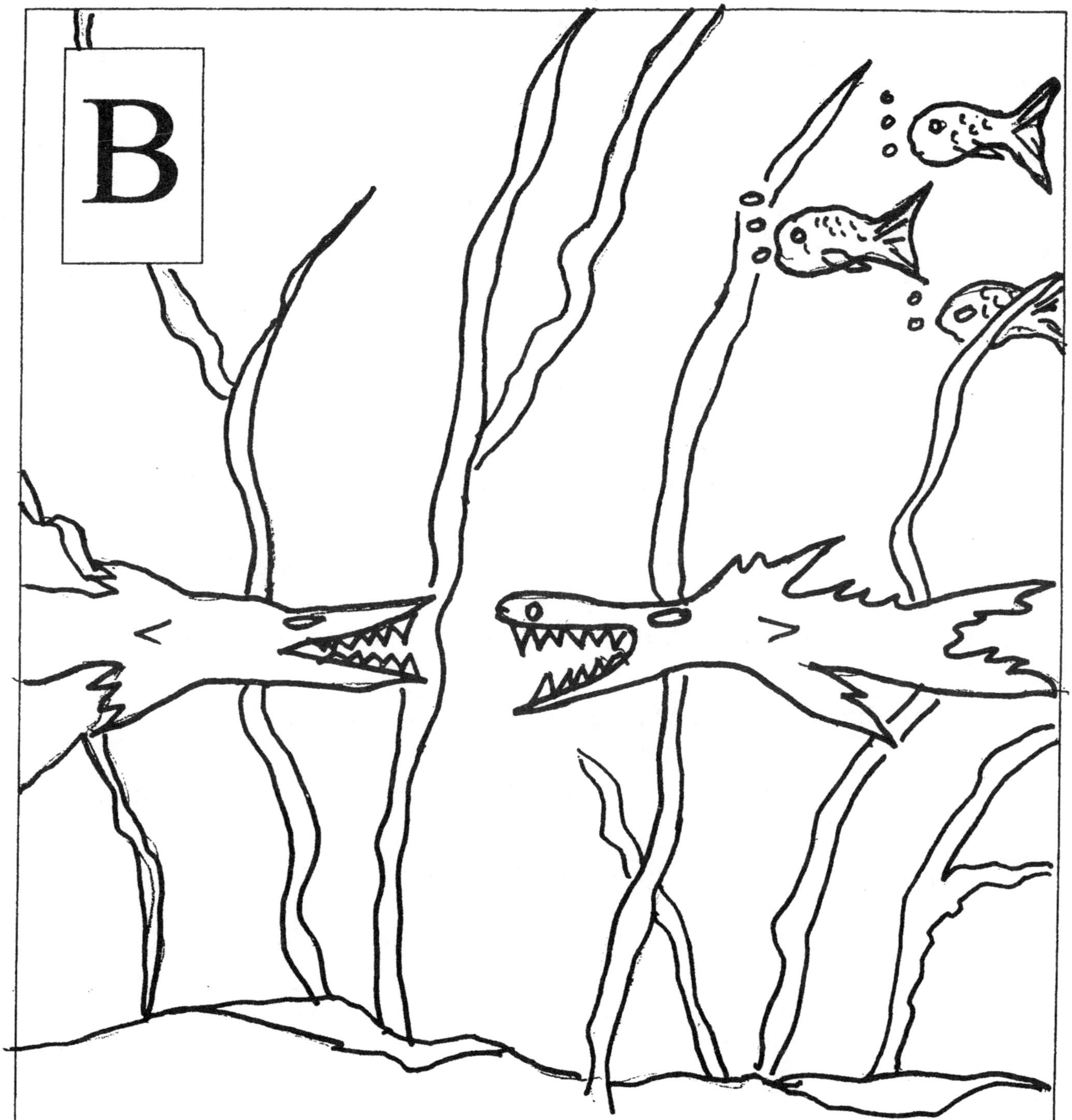

Barnaby Barracuda can cause fierce fear
to any daring diver who swims too near.

Cheetah

Cheetahs are part of the large cat family and live mostly in Africa. Their coat is dotted with a yellowish-brown color. These felines are meat-eaters, and they usually hunt down antelopes as their favorite meal. Cheetahs are speedy; they can run fifty to seventy-five miles per hour. That is as fast as a car! Wouldn't it be fun to see a Cheetah racing across the African plains!

"Cheetah." The World Book Student Discovery Encyclopedia. 2000. Vol. 3. p. 79.

**Charlie Cheetah chases his prey.
He runs so fast that his victims pray
that in a tall tree he will always stay.**

Dugong

What a strange name the dugongs have! They live in the coastal waters of the South Pacific and Indian Ocean. While grayish and brownish in color, they look a lot like a walrus. Only the male dugong's tusks show. Adult dugongs weigh around six hundred pounds and measure about six feet long. These animals are still hunted for their hides, fat, bones, and meat. People should find a way to protect the dugongs or they could become extinct.

Dugong." World Book Millennium 2000. Vol. 5 p. 379.

D

Dougie Dugong is so enormous
he should go on a diet.
Since he weighs six hundred pounds,
he should really try it!

Emu

Emus are the second largest birds in the world, and they are found mostly in Australia. They weigh up to one hundred pounds and stand a little over five feet tall. Since they weigh so much, they can't fly, but they can run really fast on their two long legs. Another interesting fact is that female emus lay ten eggs that are green on top. Male emus get the job of sitting on the eggs until they are hatched. Lucky Dad! Their diet consists of green plants and various fruits. This causes them to be considered pests by many Australian farmers because they destroy sheep fences and eat crops. Even though some people call them "pests," I think that they are fascinating animals.

"Emu." World Book Millennium 2000. Vol. 6. p. 264.

E

Emily Emu will never fly high,
but with supersonic speed she
passes other animals right on by.

Flamingo

Flamingos are tall, skinny-legged birds with a long neck and curved beak. They have beautiful red or pale pink feathers with sometimes black tips. No wonder people like to paint pictures of them! These birds stand three to five feet tall. Flamingos live in groups called colonies which can have thousands of members. They mate once a year and lay one egg in a nest made of mud. It takes thirty days for an egg to hatch. Living in marshes, lakes, and seas, they eat algae and shellfish. They use hairs that are on the edge of their beaks to strain sand and mud from the food that they catch. Flamingos live fifteen to twenty years in their own habitat, but when they are in captivity they will live longer.

"Flamingo." World Book Millennium 2000. Vol. 7. p. 226-27.

F

**Florence Flamingo is pretty in pink.
But as a lawn sculpture she's silly, I think.**

Gorilla

Gorillas live in the rain forests of Africa. They look like big monkeys and some people think the gorillas are scary and mean. Maybe those people saw the movie "King Kong." Actually, gorillas are very gentle creatures. Bark, leaves, and fruit are their favorite food. Did you know that scientists have been able to teach a gorilla how do sign language? How amazing!

"Gorilla." The World Book Student Discovery Encyclopedia. 2000. Vol. 5. p. 70.

Gloria Gorilla thinks she is a gorgeous gal.
To all the boy baboons she wants to be their pal.

Hyena

Hyenas can be found in different parts of Africa and Asia. Sometimes their fur has stripes, and sometimes it has spots. The color is a yellowish gray. These mammals are meat eaters and are great hunters as they skillfully attack other animals for food. Hyenas have a nickname which is "laughing hyena." They got this nickname because when hyenas howl they sound like a person who is laughing. I wonder what they think is so funny?

"Hyena." The World Book Student Discovery Encyclopedia. 2000. Vol. 5. p. 208.

Harold Hyena says, “Ha, Ha, Ha!”
with a hilarious grin.
Any laughing contest he would surely win.

Iguana

Iguanas are a type of green lizard that can grow up to six feet long. They live in Mexico and several countries in South America. A favorite habitat of these animals is in trees near water. There is a good reason for this. When iguanas are attacked, they jump from their branch into the water and remain there until danger passes. However, if this doesn't work, they use their tail as a lash or whip. Another interesting fact is that the female iguana will travel as far as two miles to find just the right place to lay her eggs. She will dig a tunnel and lay as many as seventy-five eggs. Each family will certainly have a lot of little lizards leaping around!

"Iguana." World Book Millennium 2000. Vol. 10. p.50.

Ike Iguana will not win a beauty contest since he looks profoundly prehistoric at best.

Jackrabbit

Jackrabbits live mainly in Wisconsin, USA and in Canada. This type of rabbit does not look like the cute, furry Easter Bunny that appears on cards, nor does it look like rabbits found in gardens, yards, and woods. Jackrabbits are bigger. Some of them measure as big as twenty-seven inches long and can weigh up to eight pounds. Jackrabbits come in four types: white-tailed, white-sided, black-tailed, and antelope. They like to eat leafy plants that have big, thick stems. Eagles, bobcats, coyotes, and badgers are the jackrabbit's enemies. Their defense against these animals is their strong hind legs which allow them to take off to safety really fast. Do you think that a jackrabbit can out run a cheetah?

"Jackrabbit." World Book Millennium 2000. Vol. 11. p.3.

Jasper Jackrabbit is certainly not an Easter Bunny. The thought of him carrying juicy jelly beans is jokingly funny.

Kangaroo

Kangaroos hop about mostly in Central, Southern, and Eastern Australia where they survive on grass and other small plants. Covered in red or gray fur, these mammals have some unique characteristics. First, they do not carry their babies a long time inside of them like most mammals; instead, the babies complete their development in the mother kangaroo's special body part called a "pouch." Secondly, the baby is called a "joey" and is only one inch long when it is first born. Maybe a better name for this baby kangaroo would be "shorty."

"Kangaroo." World Book Millennium 2000. Vol. 11. p. 213-215.

Kara Kangaroo puts on great jumping shows while hopping and bopping to all the tunes she knows.

Lion

Deep in the southern parts of Africa lions dwell. They are strong, powerful meat-eaters who attack animals such as antelopes. The lion's roar can be heard from many miles which must frighten the other animals. Lions live in a large, family-like group called a "pride." Female lions will give birth when they are three or four-years-old. When their babies, which are called "cubs," are just two-years- old, they are chased away from their pride and have to survive on their own. This may sound mean, but it is necessary so that the cubs can grow up to be brave and strong. I wonder if the adult lions are proud of their pride?

"Lion." The World Book Student Discovery Encyclopedia 2000. Vol. 6. p. 200.

L

Ludwig Lion keeps the jungle animals awake at night.
His roaring and snoring even causes creepy crawlers great fright.

Moose

Moose, not "mooses" or "meese," live in the forests of northern regions of the United States and Canada. These animals with blackish-brown fur are quite big and strong, but they do not attack animals for food. They prefer shrubs and twigs to eat. One of the most interesting features of moose is the males' huge antlers that look too big for their head. In the winter they shed these huge head pieces, but in the spring the antlers grow back. This is a good thing because moose use these strong antlers for defense against enemies. It may be hard to believe, but a whole wolf pack cannot kill a fully-grown healthy moose when he defends himself with his powerful antlers.

"Moose." The World Book Student Discovery Encyclopedia. 2000. Vol. 7. p. 147.

M

Morris Moose's awesome antlers
are some of the best.
Stunning and strong,
they pass the toughness test.

Newt

Newts are small amphibians which mean that they live on both land and in water. They have four legs and a slim body. Adult newts lay their eggs in the spring on underwater leaves. Three to five weeks later baby newts will hatch. However, they cannot go on land yet because they have to wait in the water for their lungs to develop. While they are living in the water, they breathe with gills. Their long wait in the water pays off because now they can go on land. Newts live on land for seven years, and then they go back to the water to mate and to raise a family of their own. I wonder how they know when seven years have passed?

"Newt." World Book Millennium 2000. Vol. 14. p. 388.

Nelson Newt has never been called "cute."
But he is nice and kind-never a nasty brute!

Octopus

Octopuses or octopi are ocean creatures with two big staring eyes attached to a fat body. With eight long tentacles or arms reaching out from all sides of their body, they are quite an unusual sight. The largest kinds of octopuses can actually grow to twenty feet wide with their tentacles stretched out. Whales, seals, and other types of fish like to eat octopuses. The most fascinating thing about octopuses is how they cleverly escape from their enemies. When they feel threatened, they can change color to match their surroundings, and then they squirt a black liquid to hide themselves. I imagine that many children would probably like to have this skill so they could hide from their brothers or sisters. Some people enjoy eating dried octopuses. Do you think that sounds tasty?

"Octopus." The World Book Student Discovery Encyclopedia. 2000. Vol. 8. p. 107.

O

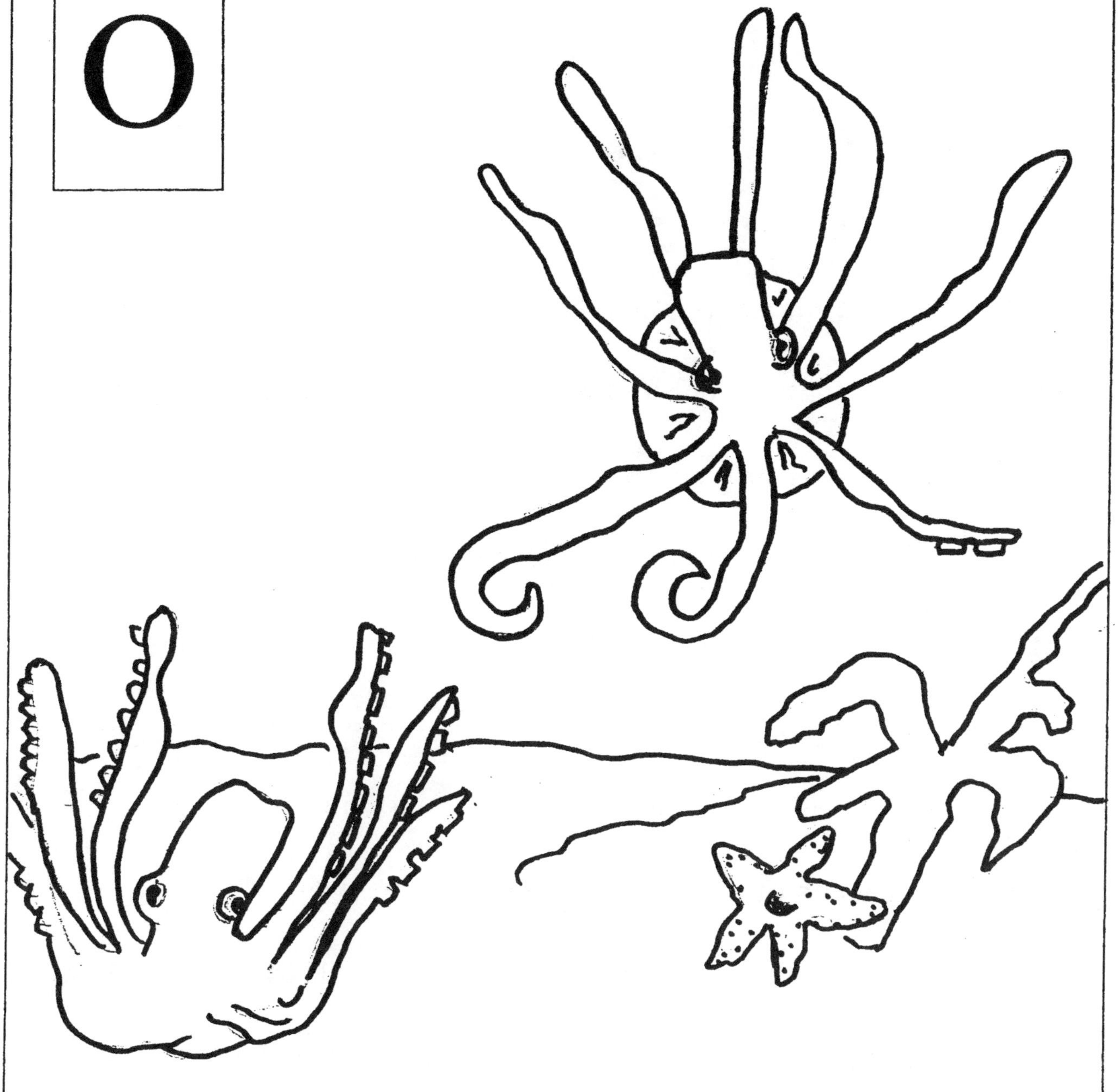

Oliver Octopus releases jet black ink.
Then he turns and swims away
as quick as a wink.

Pronghorn

Pronghorns are mammals that are native to North America. Although they look similar to antelopes and deer, they are not related. Some are white while others are reddish-brown or tan. It is easy to tell the male pronghorn from the female. The male's horns may grow ten to eighteen inches in length, but the female's horns are just stubs, if she has any horns at all. In the Western Hemisphere, pronghorns are said to be one of the fastest land animals. They can run as fast as sixty miles per hour! My family and I got to know the pronghorns well when we were stationed at F.E. Warren Air Force Base in Cheyenne, Wyoming. They roamed freely throughout the base, and they were very tame and friendly animals.

"Pronghorn." World Book Millennium 2000. Vol. 15. 818-819.

P

Paul Pronghorn looks much like a darling deer.
He roams the Wyoming plains with many steer.

Quail

Measuring larger than a sparrow and smaller than a buzzard, quail belong to the family of partridges, pheasants, and turkeys. Adult quail grow to be eight to twelve inches. Forty-five different species of quail exist. They are a favorite bird for both hunting and food. Finding quail would be quite simple since they live on all the continents except Antarctica. In North America the best known type of quail is the bobwhite. Interestingly, when bobwhites calls, it sounds as if it is actually saying, "bobwhite." As most birds, the female quail has bland colors of gray, tan, or brown. The males' feathers, while brown in color, contain attractive patterns of white, blue, black, or reddish-brown. A unique behavior of quail is that they gather together in the fall and winter into groups called, coveys. Perhaps they do this for protection in hopes of not becoming someone's Christmas dinner.

The World Book Student Discovery Encyclopedia. 2000. Vol. 9. p. 163.

Q

Quinterra Quail tells quite a tall tale about hundreds of hunters she has eluded without fail.

Rhinoceros

Picture this, an enormous gray animal with wrinkles and two horns sticking out from the top of its nose. The rhinoceros, or "rhino" for short, is one of the largest land animals. It can grow to weigh as much as two thousand pounds and tower up to six feet tall. Home for the rhinoceros include: Africa, Southeast Asia, and on several islands off the coast of Asia. The huge horn is used for protection from enemies. Sadly, man is one of the rhino's enemies because some people kill this creature just for their horn. So many rhinos have been killed that they are in danger of becoming extinct.

"Rhinoceros." World Book Millennium 2000. Vol. 16. p. 293.

R

Richard Rhinoceros resembles an ancient guy.
He'd pass for stegosaurus should he want to try.

Stork

Storks are interesting-looking birds with long, skinny legs and pointed beaks that look like fishing poles. Fourteen species of storks live in the Eastern Hemisphere, and three other species live in the Western Hemisphere. Standing about three and one-half feet tall, many storks can be found in Florida swamps. Frogs, insects, fish, and small mammals are storks' favorite foods. Although many drawings on greeting cards can be seen showing a stork bringing a baby home to its parents, this is simply not true. This is just an old story.

"Stork." World Book Millennium 2000. Vol. 18. p. 911.

S

Stella Stork fancies fishing with her long beak.
To seek her supper, she must silently sneak.

Tapir

Tapirs are very unique-looking animals that live in Central and South America, the Malayan Peninsula, and Sumatra. At first glance, they look a lot like huge pigs, but their nose looks like a short elephant's trunk. Tapirs' hides range in a variety of colors including: black, white, or dark brown depending upon where they live. It is important for tapirs to be near water because they love to swim. Just like rhinos, they are in danger of becoming extinct because people hunt them for their hides and meat.

"Tapir." World Book Millennium 2000. Vol. 19. p. 41.

T

Tanya Tapir takes time for a drenching dip.
After splishing and splashing, the water she'll sip.

Umbrella Bird

Living in South and Central America, the umbrella bird is about the size of the common crow. The male bird is very interesting-looking. It has skin at the base of the neck called a "wattle." In addition, it has a crest of black feathers on its head that hangs down in such a way that it looks like an umbrella. People may think that this is a strange-looking bird, but these features serve a purpose. The male birds use the wattle and crest of feathers to attract a mate. I wonder if his black, feathered crest helps to keep rain off him as well as to call the attention of female birds?

"Umbrella Bird." World Book Millennium 2000. Vol. 20. p. 19.

Umbray Umbrella Bird is proud of his black crest. With this handsome headpiece, he stands out from the rest.

Vampire Bat

Vampire bats are small, bird-like animals. They can be found in damp, warm parts of North, South, and Central America. Dark places such as caves and sometimes people's attics and barns make the perfect habitat for them. They have brownish-red fur, and their front teeth are very sharp and triangular-shaped. In addition, they make a screeching sound that gives many people the chills. These creepy creatures get their name because of their behavior. Vampire bats attack and suck the blood of birds, horses, and cattle. People need to be careful not to get bitten by these bats because they may carry diseases that must be treated by a doctor.

"Vampire Bat." The World Book Student Discovery Encyclopedia. 2000. Vol. 12. p. 14.

Victor Vampire Bat is like a circus acrobat hanging upside down.
Sadly for him, he makes people shiver and frown.

Wolverine

Imagine short, furry, bear-like creatures with a bushy tail. These are wolverines. Their fur is black or brown like a bear, but they have a light band of fur on the back of their tail and along the sides. Asia, Europe, and North America are home to the wolverines. They eat plants and tiny animals such as rodents. However, in the winter when they cannot find these foods, they will track down and eat caribou and reindeer. Although they are interesting-looking animals, I doubt that wolverines would make excellent pets.

"Wolverine." The World Book Student Discovery Encyclopedia. 2000. Vol. 12. p. 115.

Walter Wolverine wanders in search of a midday meal.
A farmer's animal he might stealthily steal.

X-ray Tetra

These very small, unusual fish, called x-ray tetras, get their name from their appearance. They are almost totally transparent. Measuring only about two inches in length, they can be found in South American Rivers. As for any color, these fish may have a hint of yellow, black, and red. The female will lay as many as seventy to one hundred and fifty eggs at a time. The eggs will hatch quickly between twenty and twenty-eight hours. Interestingly, x-ray tetras have very few enemies. Some people like to include these fish in their home aquariums as pets. X-ray tetras must be interesting to watch since their inside can be seen.

"X-ray Tetra ." International Wild Life Encyclopedia.
2002. Vol. 21. p. 2998-2999.

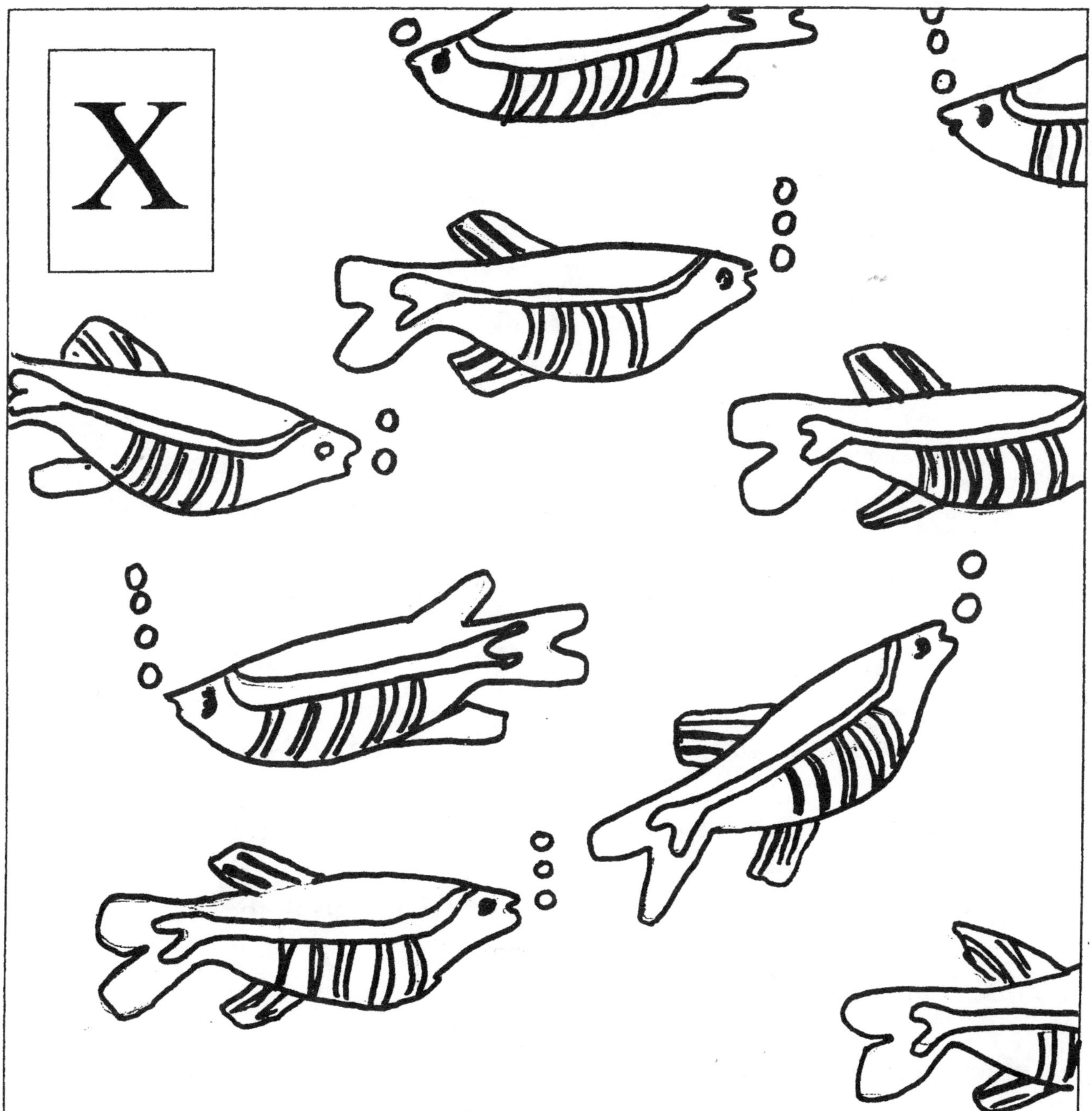

Xandra X-ray Tetra is so tremendously transparent that her yellow, black, and red colored scales are barely apparent.

Y ak

Yaks are large, bull-like animals that live in an Asian country named Tibet. Yaks prefer living on flat, high plateaus. There are two types of yaks: wild and tame. Wild yaks have blackish-brown or solid black shaggy fur covering their bodies. Tame yaks, on the other hand, are smaller and their fur is usually spotted or white. Interestingly, people in Tibet drink the milk from yaks and eat their meat just like people in the United States and other countries drink cows' milk and eat beef. Do you think that people in Tibet use the shaggy fur from yaks to make winter coats?

"Yak." The World Book Student Discovery Encyclopedia. 2000. Vol. 12. p.135.

Yolanda Yak yearns to live on an Asian plateau.
She'll never be found in a fancy French chateau.

Zorilla

A "zowhata?" That's right, a zorilla. Not many people are familiar with these African skunk-like creatures which can be found in the Sub-Saharan Desert. Their name originates from the Spanish word "zorro," which means fox. This may be because much like a foxes, they live in underground dens or burrows. Or could it be that they are very sly? Regardless, zorillas are not a member of the fox family at all; they are relatives of the weasel. These carnivorous animals eat hares, birds, snakes, and rodents. Much like the well-known skunk, zorillas spray an awful smelling musk on anything that threatens them. The nauseating odor also burns the victim's eyes, and it may last for days. Any animal or person sprayed by these creatures would probably never forget the name ... ZORILLA.

"Zorilla." Yahoo. www.pjc.cc.flc.us. retrieved February 8, 2005.

Z

Zorba Zorilla defends himself quick as a blink with a menacing musk that causes his victim to stink.

Future Researchers, Writers, and Illustrators

The following contributions were created by Nathan Lowe, age 5, and Josiah Lowe, age 4, younger brothers of Kirsten and Zachary. They dictated the information to their mother, Donya, and then created the illustrations.

Cows

Cows are animals that are mammals. They are wonderful creatures that God made. Cows are white and black and sometimes brown. They like to say, "Moo," which means they want food. Cows make milk for people to drink. The milk is for their babies too. Their babies are called calves. I am glad that God made cows. Nathan Lowe, September 14, 2004

C

Connie Cow grazes lazily in the farmer's field.
Magnificent milk she will surely yield.

Peacock

I visited a zoo. The peacocks were finding some food. They were eating dark, green leaves. The peacocks were pecking at the fence to get out, and they were pecking at each other too. The male peacocks spread out their tails to be pretty so that everyone would like them.
Josiah Lowe, October 11, 2004

P

Peter **P**eacock flaunts his feathers like a fancy fan
to show off his purple color as proudly as he can.